THE RUSSIAN REVOLUTION

History Books for Kids
Children's History

BABY PROFESSOR
EDUCATION KIDS

Speedy Publishing LLC
40 E. Main St. #1156
Newark, DE 19711
www.speedypublishing.com
Copyright 2017

In this book, we're going to talk about the Russian Revolution. So, let's get right to it!

The Russian Revolution was a revolt against government oppression, especially economic oppression. It took place in 1917 and was led by peasant people of the working class.

Soldiers Demonstration

The Romanovs

WHAT CAUSED THE RUSSIAN REVOLUTION

The Russian Revolution started as a fight for democracy, but then took a turn during the chaos of the events that unfolded. During the time before the revolution, Russia was ruled by the Czars. The Romanov Dynasty of rulers had been the leaders in Russia for over 300 years.

This monarchy was essentially a dictatorship that held the power over all the lands in Russia. The situation was not any different than when kings ruled over feudal lands during the Middle Ages. A few powerful people, the class of aristocrats, were wealthy and had all the lands and the peasants worked the land but didn't own it.

French Revolution

The working class people were poor and could barely feed themselves or clothe themselves during the brutal winters in Russia. At times, they were treated as if they were animals. They felt that nothing would improve their condition and they had lost hope. Under similar circumstances, the people of France had overturned their government, during the French Revolution, and established democracy and capitalism.

BLOODY SUNDAY

Then something happened that set the stage for the coming Revolution. A group of workers were on their way to the palace of the Czar to give him a signed petition. They simply wanted him to consider improving their working conditions. The Czar's soldiers opened fire on these workers and many were slaughtered or critically injured. This day, January 22, 1905, was called Bloody Sunday from then forward.

The Russian Revolution

The Bloody Sunday

Prior to this occurrence, many of the workers still admired the Czar, but this changed everything. After this event, he was considered to be their enemy. This fueled the desire for a revolt and a takeover of the government.

WORLD WAR I

When World War I began in 1914, Russia and Germany were at war with each other. Germany's growing strength was a threat. Even though they were a much smaller country than Russia, they were much more economically powerful. The army in Russia was made up of peasants and working class men who had been forced to fight. They had no military training at all and had no clue how to fight.

World War 1

World War 1

As if this were not bad enough, they had been forced to fight without boots for their feet, food to eat, or working weapons. They were going up against the well-trained military that Germany and the other Central Powers had. Over a three year period of time, almost 2 million of these peasant soldiers died in battle.

Another 5 million survived the war but were severely wounded. The Russians blamed their government and the Czar for getting into the battle. They had endured untold levels of suffering and their young men had been brutally killed.

February Revolution

THE FEBRUARY REVOLUTION

The February Revolution in 1917 began with a workers' strike. As the workers were gathering to begin the strike, they were discussing politics, which was a heated topic. A riot broke out. Fearing that chaos would occur, Nicholas II, the Czar, sent a command to the Russian army to shoot the people and stop the workers from rioting. However, the Russian soldiers refused to comply with the Czar's order. They wouldn't shoot the peasants and workers. Instead, they began to revolt against the Czar.

Afew days of uncontrolled riots followed as the army overthrew the Czar. He was forced to leave his position and the revolutionaries put two different political parties in position. The two groups were:

February Revolution

ПРАЗДНИКЪ ВСЕМІРНОЙ АРМІИ ТРУДА

Petrograd Soviet

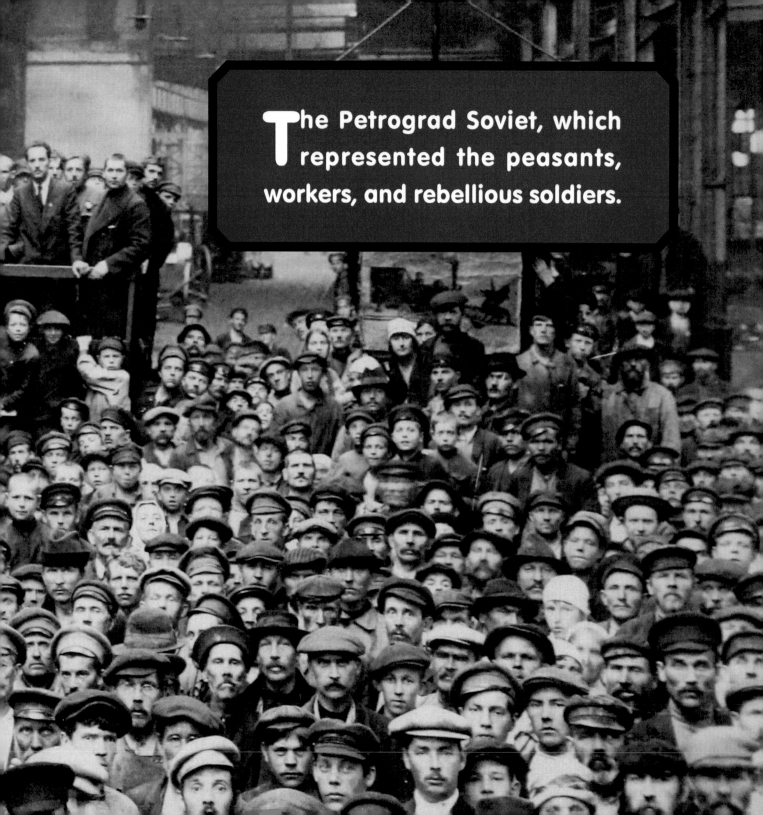

The Petrograd Soviet, which represented the peasants, workers, and rebellious soldiers.

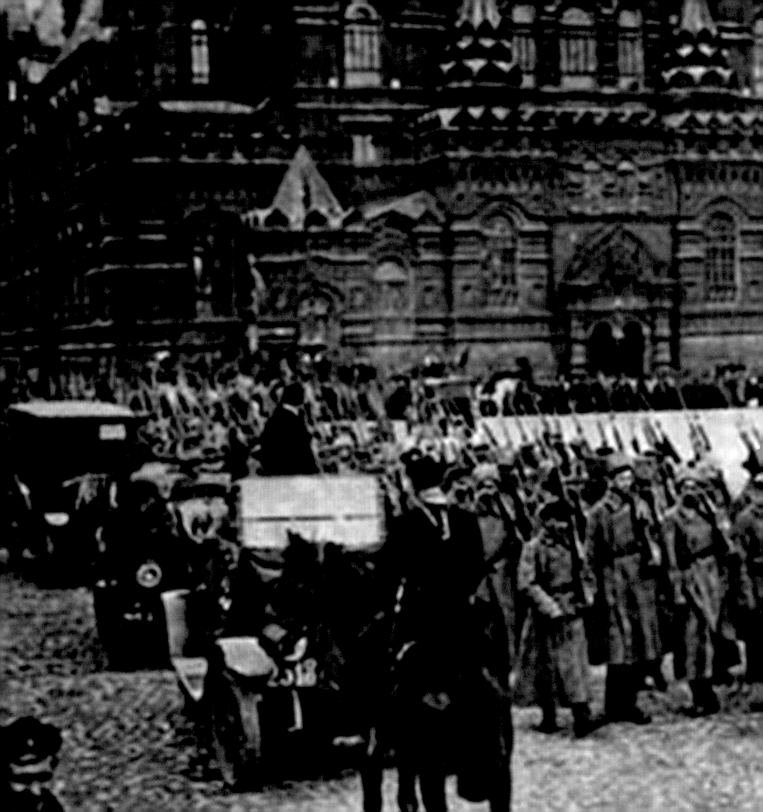

The Provisional Government, which was the former government without the Czar. After this, the country was in total chaos for some time.

Russian Revolution

Bolsheviks

VLADIMIR LENIN AND THE BOLSHEVIKS

During the time of this unrest, the revolutionary Vladimir Lenin, had been in Europe. He had been exiled by the Czarist government years before for his Marxist ideas. With the help of the German government, he now returned to Russia. Within this chaos, there was an opportunity for him to take power and put his party, the Bolsheviks, into the dominant position in Russia.

After the February Revolution, the government with its two divisions ruled the country. Lenin's party, the Bolsheviks, were one of the political groups that were part of the Petrograd section of the government. As soon as Lenin was back in the country he began to speak out about the evils of the Provisional Government.

Bolsheviks

Город Петроград
прибавка на
семьи солдат

February Revolution

He convinced the people that this government was no better than what the Czar's government had been. However, he didn't want a form of democracy or capitalism as the new government. Instead, he wanted his own form of Marxism, which was called communism, to form the new government's foundation.

BOLSHEVIK REVOLUTION

In October of 1917, Lenin had gained enough power that he and his party were able to overthrow the new government. He put the Bolshevik party in charge with himself as leader. After this Bolshevik Revolution, sometimes called the October Revolution, Russia was established as the Soviet Republic. The Soviet Republic was now the first country in the world with a communist government.

Treaty of Brest-Litovsk

LENIN BECOMES THE LEADER OF THE SOVIET UNION

Once in charge, Lenin began to transform the country with changes. He started by signing a peace treaty, the Treaty of Brest-Litovsk, with Germany. This is exactly what Germany had hoped would happen when they helped Lenin gain entrance back into Russia during the beginning of the Revolution. The Russians withdrew from the fighting.

The new government took over all the industries in Russia and began to change the economy from one that was based on farms to one that was more industrial and manufacturing. Lenin also grabbed control of the farmland that belonged to wealthy landowners and divided it up among the peasants who were working it. Women and men had equal status in this new country. Lenin was an atheist and he began to ban the practice of religion throughout the land.

Treaty of Brest-Litovsk

Bolsheviks

In addition to seizing property from landowners, Lenin had exposed hidden information regarding secret treaties that the Czars had made with other countries around the world. When World War I was over, twenty-one countries including Britain and the United States began to support a counter-revolution against the Bolsheviks. There was a real fear that communism would become a dominant force.

RUSSIAN CIVIL WAR

Despite his immense amount of power, Lenin couldn't stop the different political views in the Soviet Republic. Not everyone was happy with the Bolsheviks being in power. Many people didn't want them in power at all. From 1918 to 1920, the country broke out in a civil war. It was the Bolsheviks, called the Red Army, against the Anti-Bolsheviks, called the White Army.

Red Army

Red Army

In 1918, the United States President Woodrow Wilson sent in over 12,000 troops to join the fight against the Bolshevik Red Army. However, during the course of the fighting, the US discovered that there was little chance the White Army would be victorious. They found out that for the most part the Russian people sided with the Bolsheviks. Eventually, the United States brought their troops home and the event was thought of as one of the worst interventions in American history.

During the civil conflict, Lenin showed himself to be a cruel and ruthless leader of his people. If anyone spoke out against him or the new government, he had them immediately killed. He did exactly as the Czar had done and drafted peasants to fight in the Red Army. The food that the peasants had harvested now became food to feed the vast army of soldiers.

Red Army Soldiers

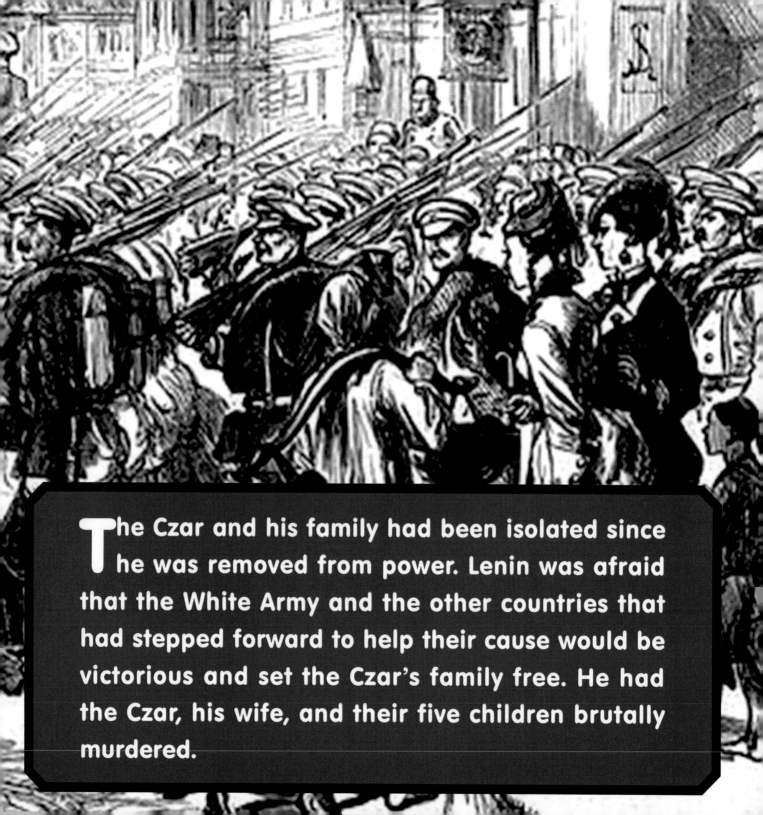

The Czar and his family had been isolated since he was removed from power. Lenin was afraid that the White Army and the other countries that had stepped forward to help their cause would be victorious and set the Czar's family free. He had the Czar, his wife, and their five children brutally murdered.

As the conflict continued, the Soviet Republic was nearly destroyed as millions of people had no food. Death by starvation was commonplace. The Bolshevik Red Army won this civil war and the country was once again renamed. This time it was named the United Soviet Socialist Republic, USSR for short, to show the supposed solidarity of the people.

The Russian Revolution

During the war between the Red and White armies, Lenin established War Communism. This meant the government essentially owned everything in the Soviet Republic. Soldiers could take anything that they needed from private citizens.

Once the war was over and the Bolsheviks were back in power fully, the country was once again in chaos. Lenin established a New Economic Policy, which allowed some private farms as well as businesses.

The Russian Revolution

The USSR lasted from 1922 until it began to collapse in the late 1980s. The country dissolved on December 25, 1991 and is now fifteen separate independent nations with different governments.

Awesome! Now you know more about the Russian Revolution. You can find more History books from Baby Professor by searching the website of your favorite book retailer.

Visit

BABY PROFESSOR
EDUCATION KIDS

www.BabyProfessorBooks.com

to download Free Baby Professor eBooks
and view our catalog of new and exciting
Children's Books